THE STUPID SH*T PEOPLE SAY

to grievers

JOHN POLO &
CAROLYN GOWER

THE STUPID SH*T PEOPLE SAY to grievers

JOHN POLO & CAROLYN GOWER

www.johnpolocoaching.com

www.carolyngowercoaching.com

This book is dedicated to our fellow grievers who are constantly subjected to stupid comments in this grief-illiterate world that we live in.

Intro from Carolyn

When I became a widow in 2017, one of the many things that I did NOT expect was the amount of stupid shit that people were gonna say to me!

Now, don't get me wrong, there have also been some beautiful people in my life … people who have continued to show up and be wonderfully supportive.

However, what I've come to learn is that …

grief makes most people feel very uncomfortable.

And this uncomfortableness causes some weird shit to come out of their mouths!

Some of the comments you're going to read in this book are extreme, and not heard every day, but most of them are very common things that grievers, including myself, have heard over and over.

Every comment that we're sharing with you is real.

And while most may be said with good intentions, they can still feel hurtful, cruel, dismissive, judgmental, and isolating to someone in the throes of grief.

It's time to change this.

Intro from John

I completely agree with everything that Carolyn just said.

Including the fact that there are people out there who are amazing, loving and absolutely supportive.

But, I do need to reinforce the truth that …

NOT EVERYTHING is said with good intention.

The reason I feel the need to expand on this point, is because I will often hear people say

"but, they mean well."

And as Carolyn just said …

SOME of them DO mean well.

BUT …

some people are just assholes!

here we go ...

"My husband is so annoying, sometimes I wish HE would die."

Jackie

About three months after my husband of 35 years died, a "friend" told me that all I needed was to **find a guy who would put my feet over his shoulders and put it to me until I lost my breath, and then I would be all good.**

Margaret

"**You're so lucky.** I'm sure he had insurance, so you can just travel and do whatever you want to do. I wish it was me," my friend said as her **LIVING**, BREATHING husband sat in the next room.

Anita

After our sweet 6-year-old was killed in a car wreck, someone told me that **it's probably for the best. He may have grown up to be a murderer or something.**

Darlene

WTF!!

WORST.

← *COMMENT.*

EVER.

I was told that I mention my late husband's name too often, and that it's become irritating.

Lynda

FACT

Your grief is likely to make some people uncomfortable. As is your healing.

Too damn bad.

#saytheirname

Two weeks after my husband died, a close family member asked why I looked so sad … REALLY??

Karen

A colleague told me **I've had a victim mindset since my wife died.**

He then went on to say that I'll **scare all of my friends away if I don't snap out of my sadness.**

It's been 5 months since the love of my life died unexpectedly.

Michael

"At least she lived a good life."

I was told this by several people
after my 57-year-old mother died.

Bernadette

I lost my husband a day after I had my lower right leg amputated. I was told he died because ...

"He wasn't strong enough to deal with you like this."

Tracie

JOHN SAYS:

And you see, honestly, this is why people's opinions of me don't even matter to me anymore.

Like, some people are just so ignorant, how can you even care what they think of you??

Before I am going to allow anyone's words, judgements or critiques of my grief or my life to impact me in any way, shape or form. I am going to strongly...

CONSIDER THE SOURCE!!

After my husband died, I was told ...

"Don't **shave your lady parts.** You don't want to be tempted to have sex now that you're single."

Megan

"Going through this will change you for the better."

Just weeks after my 13-year-old son died.

Patrick

CAROLYN SAYS:

Look, we all know that sometimes (NOT ALWAYS), people may experience post-traumatic growth after a horrible, life-changing event.

BUT … even if you do, it's something that happens over years, not weeks or months.

AND … while there may come a time when your growth feels empowering, I don't know of anyone who would not give that growth back in an instant, to have their loved one still here with them.

And then there's this ...

DO NOT give trauma the credit because you have survived the unimaginable.

DO NOT give trauma the credit for all the work you are doing every day to rebuild your life.

Common platitudes that most people *think* are helpful

(Hint: They're actually NOT)

1. "Everything happens for a reason"

2. "Time heals all wounds"

3. "Cheer up! They wouldn't want you to be sad"

4. "Just think positive and you'll be fine"

5. "They're in a better place"

Why platitude 1 stinks ...

"Everything happens for a reason"

Life can be so unpredictable. Good things happen every day. Bad things happen every day. Such is the truth of this human experience.

Telling us that our innocent child's accidental death, our sibling's suicide, or watching our spouse actively dying from cancer ... was for a reason ...

does NOTHING to help ease our pain.

There is no silver lining when someone you love dies.

And when others attempt to find one for us, it just damn hurts ...

(Like, a deep soul level kind of hurt)

Do you know why people die?

Because people die. That's why.

Why platitude 2 stinks …

"Time heals all wounds"

If you tell someone deep in grief that they'll be all healed in a given amount of time…

1) They are not going to believe you

2) This information will not make them feel better right in this moment

3) How do you know that?

Here's the thing …

Grief has no timeline.

When someone you love dies, grief is kind of a forever thing.

Grief is not like a broken toe; it's not something that you completely heal from! However, you can find healing by integrating grief into a life that feels meaningful and fulfilling to you.

After a truly profound loss, grief will change and evolve, but there DOES NOT come a day when it will magically go away.

Why platitude 3 stinks ...

"Cheer up! They wouldn't want you to be sad"

We say: If you can't be sad when someone you love dies, when can you???

Look, we agree that our dead person doesn't want us to feel so sad that we find no enjoyment in life ever again ... however, when you lose someone that you loved with all of your heart, you are gonna be sad SOMETIMES.

We will all experience many different emotions during our lifetime. It's simply not possible to be happy all of the time. All emotions are valid, and all serve a purpose.

Having someone sit with you in those harder moments, and validate your pain, is so much more helpful than someone telling you to just be happy.

You cannot cheer someone out of grief.

Why platitude 4 stinks ...

"Just think positive and you'll be fine"

Two words folks ... **TOXIC POSITIVITY!!**

Toxic positivity is when others assume that despite our emotional pain, or the difficult situation we're experiencing, we should still **only have a positive mindset.**

BUT ...

in doing this, our pain is being denied, minimized and invalidated.

When someone forces a positive outlook on our pain, they are essentially encouraging us to keep silent about whatever emotions we are feeling.

In other words, we're probably just gonna think they're an insensitive jerk and hide our grief from them!!

Why platitude 5 stinks ...

"They're in a better place"

If the grieving human believes this, that's fine.

Let them believe it.

But this is not usually a helpful thing to say to the person who is left here.

The one who now must live the rest of their life

without the person they love so much.

For even if the grieving person believes their loved one is in a better place, and that they will eventually see them again - that **DOES NOT** make up for the void of no longer having them here, *in the physical world.*

short, BUT not so sweet ...

"Aren't you over it yet?"

Every griever ever

"You deserve to be happy … just not yet."

Ashley

"Isn't it time you moved on?"

Every griever ever

When I told a former classmate of my husband's death, she said **maybe you'll find someone better.**

Beverly

"Just stay strong."

Every griever ever

"You're going to like living alone."

Nancy

"You're young.

You'll find someone else."

Way too many young widows everywhere

Carolyn says:

No human life is replaceable.

"I don't know why you're grieving so much when it was his choice to die."

My husband took his own life.

Andrea

The Stupid Sh*t People Say To Grievers

Two words that should never be said to someone who's grieving ... "AT LEAST"

There is NOTHING AT ALL that anyone can say after these two words that will ever feel helpful, or supportive, to someone who's grieving.

In fact, once these two words come out of someone's mouth, it's highly likely that the grieving person will have stopped listening before the words that follow leave the other person's mouth.

Let's take a closer look at some examples:

"At least they're not in pain anymore"

"At least you're young enough to find another partner"

"At least your children won't remember them"

"At least your children will remember them"

"At least you found true love. Some people never experience that"

"At least you got to have (any amount of time) with your person"

"At least you got to say good-bye"

"At least you didn't have to watch them suffer"

The perfect words to begin a sentence with if your goal is to invalidate another human's pain & grief experience.

Please. Just. Don't.

We say:

The words that come out of our mouths are oh-so important when talking to any human.

& especially a *hurting human.*

One of the reasons we do the work that we do is to help educate society about grief and about healing.

Because sadly, we have come to realize just how grief-illiterate our society is.

Journal Space

Stupid shit I have heard ...

_____

_____

_____

_____

_____

_____

_____

_____

_____

_____

_____

_____

_____

_____

_____

_____

_____

Journal Space

The things I WISH I had heard ...

_____

_____

_____

_____

_____

_____

_____

_____

_____

_____

_____

_____

_____

_____

_____

_____

_____

_____

_____

_____

Some helpful things to say, instead ...

People will often overthink what to say to a hurting human.

Keep it simple.

1. "I know that nothing I can say will ease your pain, and I just want you to know that I'm here to listen anytime you feel like talking."

2. "I don't know what to say, but I am here for you."

3. "I am so, so sorry."

4. "This really fucking sucks."

5. "I would love to hear memories about them, anytime you'd like to share."

6. "Whenever you need to express your emotions, I'm here to listen."

7. "It's a terrible thing you're going through. It's okay to feel sad."

8. "They loved you so much. And I know you loved them so much too."

Carolyn says...

When Tony first died, EVERYONE was telling me ...

"At least he's not in pain anymore."

And while I completely understood what they were saying, my pain felt so unseen.

I even felt guilty for feeling so sad.

But then, one friend said to me ...

"I'm so sorry, I know Tony's out of pain, but I

also know that your pain is just beginning."

And it was the first time my pain felt validated.

and now, back to the shitshow ...

I lost my only child in 2003 after childbirth. He is my everything even though I only held him for a moment. And the other day, as I was crying because I miss him and always speak about him, my own family member said to me ...

"Well, you can always adopt. You need to move on, grieving won't bring him back."

Kerries

My first husband died of colon cancer in 2008 and my second husband (who turned out to be my soulmate) died of diabetes in 2018. A medical worker said to me …

"What do you do to your husbands?"

I think she thought she was being funny.

Sharon

When I returned to work six weeks after my husband of 30 years passed, my supervisor told me ...

"You have to stop crying.

You can't come to work and cry."

He also said ...

"Your husband has a girlfriend in heaven already. He is ok, he don't miss you."

Patty

shut da fuck up

have a filter

think before
you speak!!

In front of my husband's casket, a good friend of his told me that my husband had **good taste in women** and said he wanted to **go to the closet and fuck.**

Michelle

Someone at my husband's viewing told me to contact them when I was ready to date, because **the dating world was a lot different than when I had met him.**

We were standing about two feet from the casket, and all I could think is **WTF?!**

Natalie

JOHN SAYS:

These are perfect examples of why I tell my clients that an asshole will literally hit on a widow AT THE FUNERAL.

No joke. It happens!!

On the other hand, a nice guy may struggle to approach a widow at any point, for fear of offending her.

Hint: If you're open to the thought of dating again, make sure to let people around you know. Sometimes Mr. Right might be hesitant to approach you, not knowing if the thought of dating will be incredibly off-putting to you.

"You've changed … you're not funny anymore!"

A friend stated bluntly after my sister took her own life.

Samantha

After the first anniversary of my husband's death, my sister said to me ... **"I miss the old you."**

"I do too," I sighed under my breath.

Jill

CAROLYN SAYS:

As humans, everything that we've experienced in our life up until this moment has shaped us into the person we are today.

Yes, the death of someone you love does change you.

How could it not?

Their presence in your life had an impact on the type of person you were, whether they were a partner, child, sibling, parent or close friend.

So, it makes sense that their absence would also have an impact on who you are.

And no matter how much other people might want us to go back to being the person we once were … we can't.

We have changed.

A new version of us is emerging.

You WILL continue to evolve. You WILL smile, and you WILL find joy again, but please be patient with yourself until you do.

And here's a thought ...

Instead of asking someone when they will be back to their "old self" again, maybe try spending some time getting to know who they are now.
You might just like them.

"Megan has my blessing to move on."

My husband's mother immediately after he suddenly and unexpectedly died. I hadn't even talked to the coroner yet!

Megan

It wasn't what they said that hurt.
It was the disappearing act. *Family.*

I learned that I can choose my family.
Just like I choose my friends.

Losing a child can be extremely difficult at times.

Jane

So, *let's talk about the disappearing act*

When someone you love dies, it creates a ripple effect of secondary losses in your life.

Secondary loss can be many things, including the people in your life.

We've already established that grief can make people feel very uncomfortable … and given that most people will do whatever they can to avoid an uncomfortable situation, they may, whether intentionally or not, pull the disappearing act.

Sadly, this can mean that there may be some people who won't have the same presence in your life that they once had.

While there's many reasons people may vanish after your loss, it's not all bad news…

You may be surprised by those who will unexpectedly step up and be there for you … and quite often, beautiful new friendships are formed as your circle begins to expand again.

a few grief quotes ...
by John Polo

We can grieve as we
move forward **&**

We can move forward
as we grieve

Grief is SO damn weird.

It's like, you can be doing just fine. Having a good day.

Then you're in the grocery store. & you pass the tomatoes.

All of a sudden, it hits you. Sadness.

Because she loved tomatoes.

So now you're all sad and lonely. Just standing there. Staring at the tomatoes. Wondering why your person can't still be alive.

Standing next to you.

The realization of everything that you lost comes crashing down once more.

As a kind looking human walks up next to you and grabs – a tomato – you remember what life was like when a tomato was just a tomato. & did not have the ability, *to take your breath away.*

Survive first. Exist second.
LIVE 3rd

Grieving people ARE NOT looking for special treatment.

We just ask that you not make our life more difficult **than it already is.**

My wife was AMAZING.

Absolutely amazing.

But the truth is she is not the only amazing woman to ever be born. As I hope to fall in love again one day, I don't compare new love interests to her.

That would be a disservice to them.

To me. **AND to her.**

She was 1 in 7 billion. Just as I am. Just as you are.

There will never be another Michelle. Just as there will never be another John.

Or another "John & Michelle".

When looking for love again I'm not looking for another Michelle.

I'm simply looking to find another human, *who I adore.*

I SO love when people are like,

"you gotta let them go"

NO. I most certainly do not. Her love and

memory walk with me. Every. Single. Day.

If you don't believe, or realize that, that is possible.

That's on you. & that's fine.

You can believe whatever it is that you wanna believe.

But please don't preach that nonsense. 2 me.

When my spouse died, people thought that I

"just lost my spouse". As though that wasn't horrific enough.

But you were also my best friend & *my person.* People didn't realize that I lost the future that we had planned. For when you died, so did it. People didn't realize that I lost myself. My hopes, my dreams, & even for a long time, my identity. People didn't realize that my life went from one full of love, to one almost entirely void of love. People didn't realize when you died, that my life was shattered into 50 billion tiny pieces. & NOW, some people don't understand why I'm so proud of myself … or protective of my peace.

But once you've walked through hell, the fresh air of living again – feels oh SO sweet.

10 short grief quotes by Carolyn Gower

1. Healing after the death of your loved one does not require your grief to end. Healing is finding ways to integrate your grief into a life that once again feels fulfilling to you.

2. What you think of the way I grieve is none of my business. READ THAT AGAIN.

3. My grief is not fixable, and I am okay with that ... so please, can you be too?

4. Grief is so much more than the pre-widowed version of me could EVER comprehend.

5. Things that once felt important can seem so trivial after your person dies ... and things that were once trivial, are now so important.

6. We listen to you talk about your person, so please allow us to talk about ours. Their death didn't end our love for them.

7. I'll stop grieving when he stops being dead ... so until then, please stop asking.

8. I like who I've become. I just don't like what I had to go through to get here.

9. Your absence will always sting, but there came a time when I began to remember you more often with love than pain.

10. Once I accepted that grief would always be a part of my life, I gave myself permission to not only grieve fully, but to also live fully ... because your death has shown me just how precious and finite this life is.

alright y'all ...

Take a deep breath ... here's 15 in a row

breathe

After my husband's death, a woman at work told me she knew **exactly how I felt because her daughter didn't come home from college enough.**

Julie

My daughter died in a car accident and my boss emailed me about returning to work.

At the end of the email, he said …

"You'll get over it."

Joey

The first time I was actually having a good day and feeling somewhat human again after my husband's sudden death, I got told ...

"You've bounced back nicely."

Wendy

"I don't know why you are grieving so much, you didn't know Justin for as long as his family did."

Judy

My ex-boyfriend said ...

"I know your kid is dead, but it's been 6 months. Life goes on."

Kim

Seventeen days after my husband died, a Facebook "friend" made this comment on one of my posts:

"For GOD's sake woman, people die.

Get over it."

I was absolutely dumbfounded, and asked her …

"Are you serious? I should get over my husband dying after 17 days?"

People sure have a lot to say about a life they aren't living.

Rachel

"You're so lucky he's dead. We got divorced and I still have to see him every other weekend."

Stephanie

Less than 24 hours after my mum died, my aunt called & asked ...

"What are you doing with your mum's table? She would want me to have it."

Cindy

"At least you will be cooking for one less person now."

This person was being completely serious ... and I didn't even know him that well.

I've never been more speechless.

Tiffany

My son passed away unexpectedly at 24 years old. A police officer knocked on my door to give me the news. I had a friend tell me **she knows how I feel now about the loss of my son, since her kids just moved out.**

Danielle

"At least you don't have children."

Mind you, my husband and I were struggling with infertility. Followed closely by ...

"You have your whole life ahead of you."

I was 42 when he died.

Jennifer

I lost a lot of weight after my husband died, and a woman said to me …

"Your husband would die if he could see you now."

Lori

Two months after my husband died, I was told by a close family member that I was **really milking this widow thing**.

Crystal

I returned to work two days after my husband's funeral and had a co-worker stop by my office to offer her condolences and say **I know exactly how you feel. I had to put my dog down last week.**

Dianne

"You should be thankful that you had so many years with him."

Duh!

But that doesn't mean I am not allowed to grieve.

Penny

Okay,
let's pause here
because WE BOTH have
something to say …

 **John says...**

I am incredibly grateful for the time I had with Michelle.

But I still recognize just how cheated we were.

I feel both.

 **Carolyn says...**

Tony showed me what true, unconditional love really felt like ... **every day.**

And while I am so very grateful that we got to have six years together...

I also can't help feeling ripped off that we ONLY got to have 6 years together.

The point is ...

It's normal to feel **grateful** that they were part of our life, and for the love shared, and to still feel so damn **sad** that they died.

Gratitude and grief can co-exist.

let's change the mood
for the next couple
of pages ...

The most beautiful thing John has heard

"I have never seen a human love another human, the way that you love her."

- Michelle's cousin

The most beautiful thing Carolyn has heard

"You made Tony the happiest we've ever seen him."

- **Tony's parents**

Journal Space

Make a list of helpful, kind & beautiful things people have said to you since your person died ...

_____

_____

_____

_____

_____

_____

_____

_____

_____

_____

_____

_____

_____

_____

_____

_____

_____

No words needed ... by Carolyn

There's been many moments during my grief experience where I've felt comforted by someone without any words being spoken.

Those moments usually involved one special thing ... A HUG.

When you're widowed, human touch is something that you miss so, so much.

And while it will never replace what you're missing from your loved one, it can feel very comforting when a caring friend or family member warmly wraps their arms around you.

And I'll take it one step further by saying ... the absolute best hugs come from other widowed people! IYKYK.

It's like an unspoken bond ... an immediate deep connection that you share.

Yep, widowed peeps sure do give the best hugs!

No words needed ... by John

It was Memorial Day.

I can't remember what year, but I believe it was two and a half years after Michelle died.

Life was going anything but my way, and I felt as though I was hanging on by a thread.

The day before the holiday, something happened which put me over the edge. And then, waking up that morning to a beautiful May day which the world would be spending with their loved ones, when my person was dead - felt like a pain too great to bear.

I can remember that morning sobbing in the mirror. Just sobbing. Uncontrollably, and without the ability to stop. I no longer wanted to be here ... at all.

An hour later, with swollen eyes and a shattered heart, I drove to my sister's house for the family grill out.

Upon pulling up to the house, I could not go in. The tears were still falling from my eyes, and I did not want to be around other people. Especially when everyone else there had a living, breathing spouse.

I turned the car back on and drove a few blocks away to where there was a vacant hotel still standing. I parked there and sobbed for about another hour, wondering how this had become my life.

Finally, I collected myself enough to drive back to my sister's house and walk up to the front door where my family was gathering.

As I rang the bell and my sister opened the door, I said not a word. I simply motioned for her to come with me into her bedroom, which was to the left of the front door. Upon entering the bedroom, I began to sob again. Some of the absolute most intense tears that I had ever sobbed.

My sister, not knowing what to do or say, simply sat there with me and rubbed my back. She didn't try to do anything. She didn't try to say anything. She simply sat there with me. Seeing my pain. Hearing my pain. And respecting my pain. She simply rubbed my back.

In that moment, that is exactly what I needed.

4 Things We Need
You to Know

1. People are a version of self-care.

& a REALLY, REALLY important version, at that!

The people in your life are going to have a huge impact on your grief AND on your healing.

Surround yourself with people who lift you up; those who will see, hear and validate your pain. People who are going to respect how you grieve, without judgement. People who make you laugh, and who understand that there will be moments in which you cannot laugh. Surround yourself with people who cheer you on.

IT MATTERS.

2. Build your support network.

Something that non-grievers often don't recognize is that it's not just the loss of your loved one. There is also a TON of secondary losses.

Sadly, one of those losses is losing some of the people who have been a part of your life. Some people will step UP and some will step AWAY, and it will most likely be the ones you least expect.

The good news is that you can meet beautiful new people who will play a big part in your healing journey.

The power of a grief community should never be underestimated. Connecting with others who are on the same path as you, and truly understand, can be a deep, life-changing experience. This can be in the form of grief groups (both in-person and online), group grief coaching programs or workshops, support meetings or social outings for grievers.

Finding that deep connection might come from someone in your community who has had a similar type of loss, or even someone from across the globe. If grief is now in your life and you aren't yet part of a community, please seek out what is available either online or in your local area.

The thought of it may be intimidating at first; however, the upside of such connections can be truly profound.

3. "Let me know if there's anything I can do."

This is something that's said to grievers on a regular basis; however, when we are grieving, we often don't even know what we want or need at any given moment. So how are other people supposed to know?

A tip for the griever: As things you need pop into your head, write them on a list. Keep that list with you, so when someone asks, you can give them the option of choosing something suitable.

A tip for the support person: Offer something specific. Think of three things that you could potentially do for your grieving friend and let them choose. Some suggestions could be to drop off a cooked meal, arrange a food delivery, walk the dog, school pick-up, mow the lawn or take their children to the playground.

Think of what might be helpful to them. And remember, sometimes what a grieving person might want the most is for you to simply sit with them, talk to them, and allow them to pour out their heart and speak about their deceased loved one freely - and to hear you speak about their deceased loved one, too.

4. Protect your peace.

For so many of us, after the hell we've been through, PEACE becomes our number one priority. If there are people in your life who aren't there for you, are critical of the way you grieve, or say stupid, hurtful comments, consider your options:

- Do you need to speak up and tell them how they have let you down or hurt you?

- Is it time to put boundaries in place?

- Will you lower your expectations of how they support your grief, and focus on the value they otherwise bring to your life?

- Or does it make more sense to just say "**fuck this**" and walk away?

Think about each situation individually and decide what is going to be best for YOU. Focus in on your PEACE. Grieving and rebuilding are hard work. There is a built-in level of exhaustion that comes with this type of pain.

So, ask yourself: Are they worth it??

there's still
plenty more poop
to come …

"You're dating again?

You never really did love him, did you?"

Becca

"If you keep talking about Steve so much, nobody else is ever going to want you."

Katie

"You're going to be so lonely now."

Emma

A friend told me I need to **schedule my rough days, and I should only be allowed 2 or 3 rough days a month.**

Mary

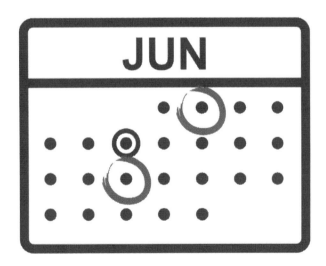

My sister said ...

"I know how you feel.

I have had nightmares
about my husband dying."

Teryl

"I can relate, my husband is travelling for work this weekend, so I'm a solo parent till Monday."

Jaimie

At my husband's viewing a hospital co-worker said to me,

"He's so pale."

Nancy

"I know he was happy with you, but he'll be **so much happier** to be with Jesus now."

Kendra

"He didn't believe in God. So, he's in hell now."

Michelle

"God must have needed him more."

or

**"God doesn't give you
more than you can handle."**

Both hurt so bad when my husband died.

I heard them over and over again.

Vicky

JOHN SAYS: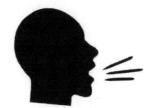

"God needed her more" is probably the platitude that bothers me the most. Like, please – *just stop.*

He is the almighty.

I am a living breathing human.

He would have been just fine without her.

I'm PRETTY DAMN SURE that I needed her more.

People don't realize how their words hurt …

But as grown-ass adults, they should!

Widowhood vs Divorce

After your spouse or partner dies, people will compare your widowhood to their divorce ... all the time!

In fact, it's one of the comments that our widowed clients tell us they dislike the most.

So, we decided to share our personal experiences about this with you ...

Carolyn's thoughts:

Hmmmm … the old divorced versus widowed comparison.

In a nutshell … it is never helpful to compare grief AT ALL, but especially not this one.

Both parties are likely to walk away feeling frustrated and misunderstood.

As it happens, I have experienced both, so I do feel somewhat qualified to talk about this.

Divorce is horrible and painful and life-changing.

Widowhood is horrible and painful and life-changing.

You will grieve as a divorcee.

You will grieve as a widowed person.

In MY OWN experience, the difference lies in the fact that someone you still loved and wanted to spend the rest of your life with, is dead. **They died.**

In divorce, apart from both partners still being alive, at least one of the couple has decided to end the relationship. If that's not you (as was in my case), that can be very painful.

However, as hard as that was for me (and it was extremely hard), it was very DIFFERENT from watching Tony DIE.

The pain of watching someone I loved with all of my heart take his last breath … knowing how desperately he wanted to live, knowing how hard he fought for our dream of growing old together … that was **gut-wrenching.**

Divorce ends a relationship.

Death ends a life, not a relationship … and it definitely doesn't end your love for them.

After divorce, most often you will get over the break-up in time … however, when your person dies, it's common to grieve for **the rest of your life.**

Then there's this …

If you have children together:

After divorce, your children still have a living parent to help raise them and make the big decisions.

Widowed parents don't have that… and being a solo parent to grieving children while also grieving yourself, is **extremely hard.**

So, please just do not compare.

It really serves no purpose whatsoever.

An important message

While we're on this topic …

Please never, ever call a widowed person's deceased partner their **ex.**

We did not break up with them … they died.

John's thoughts:

While I have never been divorced, I have had my heart BROKEN by another human by choice, not death.

I started dating Michelle when I was 17 years old, and I knew very early on that I wanted to spend the rest of my life with her.

I loved her SO much.

When she ended it with me after a year, I was beyond devasted.

I could have married her back then and spent the rest of my life blissfully happy.

Losing her that first time was HORRIBLE. Truly, it was HORRIBLE.

And the truth is, that was a CHOICE. That she made. To not be with me anymore.

What's my point?

While I understand that widowed people HATE when divorced people compare their loss to ours – and I DO TOO – the truth is losing someone you love with all your heart is hell.

For every divorced person who could not wait to get out of a loveless marriage, there is one who was shattered when the person they still loved decided to leave.

So, yes – I too hate it when people compare their divorce to my wife's death, but I also realize it is possible to be completely heartbroken by the end of a relationship. Even when it does not end because of a death.

Before we continue:

Please know that this book isn't intended to beat anyone up

These people did it to themselves with the words that they have spoken!

There's stupid and then there's downright mean ...

What's the difference?

Stupid is, for the most part, excusable.

We have ALL said something stupid at some point in our lives.

And most of us have even said something stupid to someone grieving in the past (we're both grief coaches now, but we're the first to admit that we've both said stupid shit to grievers before we knew better).

Saying something stupid means you didn't mean any harm… in any way, shape or form. And that – hopefully - you want to learn to do better.

Saying something mean is completely different.

It's not really giving a damn what comes out of your mouth.

It's when a human speaks with the intent to hurt, or without consideration of how their words might hurt.

Because they are an asshole.

To be honest, we easily could have made this book – like – 4,000 pages long. The stupid & mean shit people say to grievers really is never-ending.

But ... for our own sanity and yours, we decided that this is probably enough absurdity for one book.

Journal Space

Write a letter to someone who said something stupid or mean to you ...

_____

_____

_____

_____

_____

_____

_____

_____

_____

_____

_____

_____

_____

_____

_____

_____

_____

_____

See our pain.

Hear our pain.

Validate our pain.

That's all we ask.

Sit with us in our pain.

Do not … I repeat … DO NOT try to fix us or minimize our pain.

Sometimes we need to talk about it. Let us talk.

Sometimes we need to cry. Let us cry.

This is grief.

R.E.S.P.E.C.T.

(You just sang that in your head, didn't you?)

Respect our pain.

That is absolutely the most IMPORTANT thing you can do when another human is in pain.

Even if you cannot understand it.

*In fact, we do not **expect** you to understand it.*

But we do expect you to RESPECT IT.

Carolyn says…

Sometimes it's not just words that help.

After Tony died, one of my friends would send me a text message most mornings.

She knew there were no words capable of taking my pain away, so quite often there were no words in the message … just emojis.

But … those simple emojis let me know that someone cared about me in that moment.

Those messages helped me to get out of bed many times in those very early days.

John says…

Before my wife passed, I thought *perhaps* I could envision what that felt like … to lose a partner.

I thought, *perhaps* I could put myself in their shoes.

NOPE.

Empathy is an amazing thing. But what I thought it was like, was nothing compared to the agony of the reality of what I endured.

I had not one damn clue.

Journal Space

I forgive you ...

(Hint: Forgiving someone does not necessarily mean you need to welcome them back into your life)

_____

_____

_____

_____

_____

_____

_____

_____

_____

_____

_____

_____

_____

_____

_____

_____

Journal Space

I cannot forgive you ...

_____

_____

_____

_____

_____

_____

_____

_____

_____

_____

_____

_____

_____

_____

_____

_____

_____

_____

JOHN: Carolyn, do you think we should?

CAROLYN: C'mon Johnny Poo, we have to!

JOHN: But it's already in my first 3 books!

CAROLYN: Oh, suck it up buttercup!!

Sit down and shut up

By John "Johnny Poo" Polo

Sit down.

And shut up.

Serious question: Is your spouse 6 feet under? Oh wait, are they a pile of ashes?

No.

They aren't?

Wow.

Okay. Cool.

Then, sit down.

And shut up.

My wife's name was Michelle. She's gone.

Once a widow. Always a widow.

Once a widower. Always a widower.

No, this is not a plea for sympathy.

No, these are not angry words. These are honest words.

These are passionate words.

These are real words.

Sit down. And shut up.

Unless you watched your spouse die. Unless you buried your spouse. Unless you burned your spouse.

Sit down.

And shut up.

Do not tell a widow or widower how they should be living.

Do not tell a widow or widower how they should be acting.

And please, for the love of all that is right in this world, PLEASE do NOT tell a widow or widower when they should try to love again.

I am sick of seeing widows and widowers vilified for trying to pick up the pieces of their lives.

I am sick of seeing widows and widowers vilified for trying to find companionship again.

For trying to find love again.

Hell, for trying to find ANYTHING again!

We are lost souls. On a journey to find our self again.

And YOU want to judge?

You?

Do you know the courage it takes to go back out there after your spouse has died?

After you watched them die of cancer. Or a massive heart attack. Or suicide.

After you watched them fall to 60 pounds. Having bowel movements on themselves. Having horrific hallucinations so bad that seeing them like that strangled your soul.

After you watched them fall to their knees. And clutch their chest. And take their last breath.

After you walked in on their body. Dead. Because they took their own life.

You have no idea.

Do you have any idea how badly the loss of a spouse messes with your mind? With your heart? With your soul?

No. You don't.

So, sit down.

And shut up.

You are not allowed to judge.

You are not allowed to pass judgment as you drive home to your spouse.

You are not allowed to pass judgment as you cuddle up on the couch with your spouse.

You are not allowed to pass judgment as you have sexy time with your spouse.

You. Are. Not. Allowed. To. Pass. Judgment.

Sit down.

And shut up.

Stop judging.

Stop thinking that you know what the Hell you are talking about.

Because you do not.

Your life wasn't ripped from you.

Your future wasn't destroyed.

Sit down.

And shut up.

This was not our choice.

This was not a breakup. Stop comparing.

This was not a divorce. Stop comparing.

This was not the loss of a grandpa. Stop comparing.

This was not the loss of Uncle Thomas. Stop comparing.

And, for Heaven's sake, this was NOT the loss of your damn CAT. Stop comparing!

This was the loss of a soul mate.

Our other half.

Our life.

Our love.

Our future.

Sit down.

And shut up.

The next time you see a widow or widower try to pick themselves up, dust themselves off and 'Get back out there'…

You have 2 choices.

You can either sit down and shut up,

Or…

You can give them a standing ovation.

For their heart. For their courage. For their bravery.

Those are your 2 options.

And your ONLY 2 options.

Because. You. Do. Not. Know.

- Rant. Over –

Mic Drop.

A STANDING OVATION FOR Y'ALL

Some words from Carolyn...

They Do Not Know

They do not know ... What it's like to wake every day only to relive the pain of remembering that your soulmate is dead

They do not know ... That grief is exhausting, and some days it can take every ounce of your energy just to get out of bed and keep putting one foot in front of the other

They do not know ... That you wear a "mask" every day because you don't want people to worry about you or to judge how you're grieving... and that sometimes you can't wait to be alone, so you can take off that goddamn mask and just be yourself

They do not know ... That your random visits, phone calls or messages are because you're lonely and just want to have a conversation with another human

They do not know ... How it hurts when they say "At least he's not in pain anymore"... AT LEAST... 2 words I've grown to hate. And yes, I'm grateful that he's not in pain, but can't you see that I sure as hell am!?

They do not know ... How upsetting it is to be asked for your emergency contact... but he died, and in that moment, you can't think of anyone else who could fill that role

They do not know ... How much you miss the little things... the cuddles, the small talk and silly jokes, his snoring (yes snoring!), waking up together, eating together... EVERY LITTLE THING IS DIFFERENT!

They do not know ... that you often stay up until 3am because you just cannot get into that empty bed again

They do not know ... Just how precious memories and photos are... and the devastation you feel when you realize that there will never be any more

They do not know ... How disrespectful it feels when they compare their divorce from a husband they no longer even like to watching your husband, who you loved with all your heart, take his last breath

They do not know ... The anxiety you now feel when walking into an event alone when he should be with you... or being the only single person in your group outing

They do not know ... How hard it is seeing them being affectionate with their partner, even though you're happy for them at the same time

They do not know ... The post-traumatic stress you suffer from watching the love of your life actively dying in front of you for months on end

They do not know ... How upsetting it is when they whine about their annoying partner, when you would give anything for your partner to be here doing those annoying little things

They do not know ... How incredibly hard Sundays are… because that was our day to spend together … and now all I see is happy couples ... EVERYWHERE

They do not know ... How much it hurts when they stop talking about him because they think it will upset me. If only they knew how happy it makes me to hear them sharing stories about him, because then I know he hasn't been forgotten

They do not know ... That I sometimes catch myself feeling guilty for a moment of happiness… even though I know that more than anything, he wants me to be happy

They do not know ... How jealous I get seeing old couples together, because we'll never get to have that

They do not know ... When I'm rambling onto them about meaningless day-to-day shit, it's because that's what I'd normally share with him ... but now I can't

They do not know ... Why I "talk" to my dead husband every day

They do not know ... That it's possible to feel so strong, yet so weak, at the same time

They do not know ... That I now understand the fragility and impermanence of life, and see beauty in the simplest of things

They do not know ... How much I miss him, every minute of every day!

They do not know ... That even though I've worked hard to rebuild a life that is meaningful, there will always be times when I feel sad and miss him ... and that DOES NOT mean that I'm stuck in grief

They do not know ... How terrifying the thought of missing him and feeling this lonely for the rest of my life feels, but how equally terrifying the thought of allowing myself to find love again also feels

And do you know what? I don't want them to know ... any of it!

Because you can't really know unless you have experienced it ... and I would never wish that upon anyone.

OH NO!

we still have a
few more to go …

"At least you weren't married."

Christine

"Hopefully next time you can choose someone who's more successful."

My sister never thought my husband was good enough.

Emily

"Well, you knew he had a heart condition when you married him."

Sabrina

"You don't have to worry about what you look like anymore."

&

"You can spend whatever you like and not have to hide the bill."

Karen

"You should be over this by now."

That was from a doctor I saw **two months** after I lost the love of my life to **suicide** … after I found him and desperately tried to save him, along with the help of my two children.

Leslie

I was told my husband died both

because he was needed somewhere else more & because his work was done here.

He was 37 years old, and we had a 16-month-old daughter and a son who turned 3, two weeks before his death. *Yeah, we still needed him to be with us pretty bad.* Fuck Cancer.

Ali

I lost my husband to Covid-19 in May 2021, and the terrible things people say about Covid and my story are so mean!!

Shannon

JOHN SAYS:

I literally cannot even imagine losing my loved one in any way, and then having to hear other humans in our society speaking about how the cause of their death was fake, or even worse, that their death was fake. **4 fuck's sake.**

My sister said I should apologize to her **because my grief was ruining her summer.**

Angelica

Two days after my husband died, my mother-in-law asked me if she **could have his ashes if I met someone else!!**

Sasha

I ran into some friends at a store a few weeks after he died. We were all huggers, so I hugged each of them and we chatted briefly. I came home to a Facebook message telling me it was **no longer appropriate for me to hug her husband, since I was now a "single woman".**

Carey

Carolyn says:

Unfortunately, this is all too common for widows.

From John

"He asked me when I was going to get over my dead husband. It was our first date. I was taken aback. I could not believe that those words came out of his mouth."

"What did you say?" I asked in response.

"I told him I would never get over my husband.

I then told him that I would be moving forward with my life.

But certainly not with him."

Jayne, one of my coaching clients, then proceeded to grab her coat and immediately left the date.

"How did it make you feel when you said that and left?" I asked.

"Amazing. And empowered," she responded.

From Carolyn

"My two sisters keep telling me that I'm stuck in my grief because I still talk about my husband, Mark." my client Lisa shared with me, 10 months after her husband died.

"How does it make you feel when they say things like that?" I asked.

"I feel judged … like I'm grieving wrong, and I should be doing better than I am. It makes me feel more alone than ever, like no-one really cares or understands me anymore," she cried.

"How would you prefer they treated you?" I asked.

`"I just want them to acknowledge my pain … and to listen to me, without trying to fix me," she replied.`

Together, we made a plan that gave Lisa the confidence to convey her needs to her sisters.

At our next session, Lisa told me that she felt so empowered when sharing this with them, and she finally felt heard.

The elephant in the room

Some people might wonder if it's better just to say nothing to a person who is grieving … and to be honest, if y'all gonna say some of the stupid shit we're talking about in this book, maybe it could be?!

But on a serious note, it can be just as hurtful when someone completely avoids acknowledging our pain.

The thing is … YOU KNOW that you're going through the worst time of your life … THEY KNOW that you're going through the worst time of your life … so you're both going to feel pretty damn uncomfortable waiting to see if either of you acknowledge it.

So please, just get it out in the open.

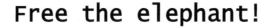

Free the elephant!

Carolyn says...

Picture this.

Your good friend Becky's husband died recently.

And understandably, Becky's been feeling pretty horrible ... so you decide to take her out to lunch in an effort to cheer her up a bit.

You both enjoy a lovely meal and a glass of wine, and you intentionally keep the conversation flowing and even get her laughing a little bit ...
but you don't mention anything about her late husband, because, well that would only remind her that he's dead and make her sad ... right?

You drop Becky off at home and feel happy with yourself for making her feel better.

Becky goes to work each day and notices that no one at her workplace ever talks about her husband, or what she's been through. This makes her feel very uncomfortable ... it's a real elephant in the room.

Then on the weekend, Becky attends a family event. Not one, not even ONE, of her family members mention her late husband's name, because they don't want to upset her either.

Becky's life has changed from being with her husband, the love of her life, every day ... to now feeling like she's not even supposed to mention his name at all to the people who she thought were closest to her!

Not only is her husband dead, but now everyone is acting like he never even existed!

How do you think Becky feels?

Let me tell you ...it's heartbreaking ... and it leaves you feeling very isolated and alone.

It's happened to me, and it happens to pretty much all widowed people ... in fact most grieving people ... EVERY DAY.

You will not remind us that our person died. We remember this every minute of every day... but when you say their name, you are letting us know that you remember that they lived.

John says...

Talk about her. **SAY HER NAME.**

Remind me of a story I already know.

Share with me a story I've never heard before.

4 when you speak of our lost loved ones you are, just for a moment, bringing their memory back to life. In full force. You are allowing us the space to feel connected to them, once more.

Journal Space

Thank you for being there for me ...

_____

_____

_____

_____

_____

_____

_____

_____

_____

_____

_____

_____

_____

_____

_____

_____

_____

Carolyn's closing thoughts

Grieving the death of a loved one is likely to be the hardest thing you will ever have to do in life. It's a pain that is unimaginable until you are forced to face it first-hand.

Therefore, it makes sense, if you are grieving, that you are going to come across people who don't know how to treat you.

While they may try their best, they just don't have the capacity to understand a pain they've never experienced.

This means that they're probably going to try and "fix" you with a meaningless platitude or offer some completely useless advice, because that's what our society has told them to do.

There will be times when you may need to put boundaries in place to protect your peace … and it's very likely that you will have to let some people go.

It's also very likely that you will find amazing support in the most unlikely of places, from people you might not have expected, or even known before.

Maybe you'll find that some of your closest friends are terrible at supporting you as you grieve.

Not everyone will have the ability to hold space for you to talk openly about your grief and emotions … and truthfully, you don't need them to.

While it is important to have someone that you feel comfortable talking to, whether it's a friend, family member, coach, counsellor or grief group, it's also important to have other people around you to fulfil your other friendship needs.

People show love and support in many different ways, so even if their grief game is a bit off, think about what value they otherwise bring to your life.

If you generally feel better after being around them …

if they're fun to have lunch, go to a movie, share a hobby or interest, or simply talk shit and have a good old laugh with …

you may want to consider keeping them in your life.

John's closing thoughts

I am going to keep this short & sweet.

You absolutely must EMPOWER yourself enough
to grieve your own way. **It is essential.**

And once you are ready to live again,
you must EMPOWER yourself enough
to LIVE your own way. **As well.**

Reading this book should have, hopefully – made it CLEAR
AS DAY, that society does not understand grief. Or healing.

It should have made it painfully obvious that some people
just be CRAY CRAY.

And with that knowledge now in hand, the next step is you
realizing that after walking through the hell you have

walked through you must **DO YOU.**

Regardless. Of. What. They. Say.

But ...

Before we go, our friend Dirk was given the **LONG-LOST SECRET** to make his grief **MAGICALLY GO AWAY ! ! !**

"Less than a year after my wife died, my *friend* told me to **go to Vegas and hire a prostitute.**

That way I could be **NORMAL** again."

This is Dirk and his amazing wife Stacey.

We hope that this book will help society do better.

For him. For her. And for all grievers *everywhere*.

Honor our pain & honor

their memory.

Please. And THANK YOU.

About the authors

John Polo

John Polo is a coach, author and speaker living just outside of Chicago, Illinois, USA.

In January of 2016, John became widowed when his 30-year-old wife, Michelle, died of cancer.

From the rubble of everything he once knew, consumed by desperation, John held on long enough until he found hope.

And he slowly rebuilt.

Today John helps others globally with grief, dating, self-growth, purpose, motivation and more, through his coaching, workshops, group programs, books, speeches, social media and the My Person Died Too podcast, which he co-hosts with Carolyn.

Find out more about John's work at: www.johnpolocoaching.com

Carolyn Gower

Carolyn Gower is a trauma-informed grief coach, certified grief educator, spiritual profiling practitioner, podcaster, author and speaker living in Ballarat, Victoria, Australia.

Carolyn became widowed when her husband Tony died from prostate cancer in 2017, aged 53. She soon discovered just how grief illiterate our society is and set out on a mission to normalize grief.

A self-confessed "grief nerd", Carolyn is now fulfilling her passion of helping other grievers across the world, through her coaching, workshops, courses, group programs, speaking, social media and the My Person Died Too podcast, which she co-hosts with John.

Find out more about Carolyn's work at: www.carolyngowercoaching.com

How this seemingly unlikely duo connected from opposite sides of the world

John and Carolyn became friends in 2019 when Carolyn decided to have a coaching session with John. It was during this session that he recognized a talent in her, asking why she wasn't also coaching. And the rest, as they say - is history!

In January 2022, John and Carolyn joined forces to launch and co-host the "My Person Died Too" podcast, where they discuss everything to do with grief and rebuilding with real vulnerability, openness and authenticity. This hit podcast is available wherever you listen to your podcasts.

John and Carolyn have also created a supportive and interactive Facebook Group called the "My Person Died Too Community" where all grievers are welcome for extra support.

LIKE OUR BOOK?

Let us know.

Post a pic or review on your social media & make sure to tag us!

#thestupidshitpeoplesaytogrieversbook

PS: And don't forget to leave us a review on Amazon!

Made in United States
Troutdale, OR
08/15/2023

12110276R00093